To Piper June, the one who made me a mama and truly believes our uniqueness is worth celebrating.

First Edition, 2023
"You are invited!"
© 2022 by MEREDITH STAGGERS
All rights reserved.

Created in collaboration with Timmy Bauer
Produced and Published by Dinosaur House
Art by Ashlee Spink

DINOSAUR
HOUSE
We Turn Industry Leaders into Kids Book Authors

www.DinosaurHouse.com

You're Invited!

Meredith Staggers

Illustrated by Ashlee Spink

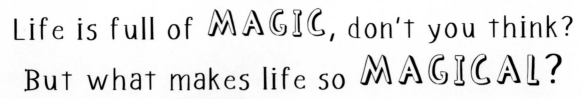

Life is full of MAGIC, don't you think?
But what makes life so MAGICAL?

The things that bring magic into my life are my **wonderful friendships.** I wish I could celebrate all of my amazing friends.

Then it hit me! I'm going to host a super fun party, with colorful balloons and sprinkle-topped cupcakes, where all of my friends are invited!

But suddenly,
I was filled with
panic!

I love all of my friends,
but they are all so different.

How could I possibly bring all my
friends together so that
everyone has fun?

Ah-HA! At my party, we'll explore each other's passions to see how alike we truly are!

Now it's time to start planning! Who should I invite?

I will definitely invite Tia. We play together on the playground every day. Since we both love crafting, she made us matching friendship bracelets!

I guess you could say,
she has a lot of CHARM.

I'm sure she would love to make decorations with me!
Now, who else?

It would hardly be a celebration without Jack! I met Jack during story time at our library. He's hearing impaired, so he brought a sign language interpreter so he could enjoy the story, too!

When story time was over, Jack taught me how to play checkers.
earning a new game from someone is a great way to make a friend.
Have you ever made a friend that way?

Ava & I met in the park and now she's one of my very best friends! Ava loves to blow bubbles and dance around them until they POP!

She would be a great addition to the party!

But she doesn't know my other friends I
plan to invite.. I wonder if she would
feel lonely...

But not if I invite Hugo!
Ava and I met him last weekend at the planetarium.
Hugo is full of really awesome facts about planets.

He told me Saturn's ring particles are made almost entirely of teeny tiny pieces of ice. Do you know any cool facts about outer space?

Musical Theatre is one of my favorite places to go after school! That's where I met Kate.

Kate's muscles work a little differently than mine, so she uses a wheelchair. But that never stops her from singing with all her heart! I think her wheelchair has superpowers!

Even though she's not able to run around the same way as some of the other kids, I think we should still invite her! What do you think?

Lee goes to my church and he designs the coolest buildings out of blocks! When he grows up, he wants to be an architect.

He taught me that architects design things like castles, bridges and towers out of real blocks! He is always teaching his friends new things, and telling silly jokes.

He would be a great guest at the party!

I met Zara at the food bank where my parents and I volunteer. She has the best ideas about helping those in need!

Last week, we organized a lemonade stand to raise money for the food bank. I bet she would be happy to help Tia and I make decorations!

Oh no! I just remembered, I'm going to need help with the cupcakes. Who could I invite that knows how to bake?

I bet him and his mom would love to make some delicious treats for the party! What kind of treats should we have?

Coco is in my gymnastics class and she's a little bit quiet. She can do the prettiest twirls on the balance beam and her fancy leotards are beautiful!

Do you ever feel shy?

Last week, Coco told me that she often feels shy when she's in a crowded room, but being around friends who care makes her feel better.

I take my dog Ruby to the dog park on Saturdays, and so does George! George is blind, which means he can't see, so he has a super smart dog named Beau who helps him get from place to place!

Ruby and I love to hear George play his drum!
Have you ever met someone who was blind?

Lola loves robots. She shows me how to make
my robots move and light up in our maker space at school!
We even created an obstacle course for them to adventure
through.

Would you ever try
building a robot?
Or dancing like one?

Levi is the MVP on our soccer team, but not many
people know he is also a talented magician! After scoring
the winning goal at our last game, Levi performed the
coolest card trick for the team!

He told us to pick a card, any card then what happened next was SO cool!

Have you ever seen a magic trick like this before?

Now that I made my invitations, it's time to hand deliver them to each guest!

"Well? How did it go, sweetie!?"

"Everyone said they would love to come! Well... Everyone except Coco. She thinks she is too shy to go to the party."

"COCO! I'm so glad you came! Now the party is complete."

"Thank you, friends, for coming today! Even though we are all different, there is a seat at the table for each and every one of us! We each have something uniquely special to contribute to this party, AND to the world."

The end.

About the Author
Meredith Staggers

Meredith Staggers, the founder of Cake & Confetti, has shared her colorful parties, mom hacks, and home decor for nearly a decade on instagram (@cakeandconfetti). She lives in Texas with her husband, Trent, and her three daughters Piper, Lila, and Dottie, and dog, Ruby (who all make an appearance in the book)!

Get some **FREE** coloring pages from this book!
Just scan the code below!

Find many more children's books on entrepreneurial topics:
www.DinosaurHouse.com/books
"We turn industry leaders into kids book authors."